Dedication

This Letters To Santa book is dedicated to all the boys and girls out there who love writing letters to Santa.

You are my inspiration for producing books and I'm honored to be a part of keeping all of your Letters To Santa.

This journal notebook will help you record your Christmas Wish List.

Thoughtfully put together with these sections to record: Dear Santa, My Name Is, I Am ___ Years Old, I Have Been and My Christmas Wish List.

How to use this Book

The purpose of this book is to keep all of your Letters To Santa notes all in one place.

This Letters To Santa journal will allow you to write your letter to Santa each and every year.

Here are examples of the prompts for you to fill in and write about your experience in this book:

1. Dear Santa
2. My Name Is - Record your name.
3. I Am ____ Years Old - Write how old you are.
4. I Have Been - Check the appropriate box: Nice, A Little Naughty But I Can Explain Or A Bit Of Both.
5. My Christmas Wish List - Blank lined space for writing or drawing your Christmas gifts you'd like to receive.

Enjoy!

Dear Santa:

My Name is:..........................

I am.......... Years old

I have been:
- ☐ Nice
- ☐ a Lil bit naughty...but I can explain
- ☐ a bit of both

My Christmas Wish List:..................

_____

_____

_____

_____

Thank You,
You are The Best Santa Ever!

Dear Santa:

My Name is:⋆⋆⋆⋆⋆⋆⋆⋆⋆⋆⋆⋆⋆⋆⋆⋆⋆⋆⋆⋆

I am............ Years old

I have been:
- ☐ Nice
- ☐ a Lil bit naughty...but I can explain
- ☐ a bit of both

My Christmas Wish List:................

_____

_____

_____

_____

Thank You,
You are The Best Santa Ever!

Dear Santa:

My Name is:⋆⋆⋆⋆⋆⋆⋆⋆⋆⋆⋆⋆⋆⋆⋆⋆⋆⋆⋆⋆

I am ⋆⋆⋆⋆⋆⋆⋆⋆ Years old

I have been:

☐ Nice

☐ a Lil bit naughty...but I can explain

☐ a bit of both

My Christmas Wish List: ⋆⋆⋆⋆⋆⋆⋆⋆⋆⋆⋆⋆⋆⋆

_____

_____

_____

_____

Thank You,
You are The Best Santa Ever!

Dear Santa:

My Name is:...........................

I am........... Years old

I have been:
☐ Nice
☐ a Lil bit naughty...but I can explain
☐ a bit of both

My Christmas Wish List:....................

_____
_____
_____
_____

Thank You,
You are The Best Santa Ever!

Dear Santa:

My Name is: ....

I am .... years old

I have been: ☐ Nice

☐ a lil bit naughty...but I can explain

☐ a bit of both

My Christmas Wish List: ....

_____

_____

_____

Thank you,
You are the Best Santa Ever!

Dear Santa:

My Name is:........................

I am............ Years old

I have been:
- ☐ Nice
- ☐ a lil bit naughty...but I can explain
- ☐ a bit of both

My Christmas Wish List:................

_____

_____

_____

_____

Thank You,
You are The Best Santa Ever!

Dear Santa:

My Name is: ....

I am .... Years old

I have been:
- ☐ Nice
- ☐ a lil bit naughty...but I can explain
- ☐ a bit of both

My Christmas Wish List: ....

_____

_____

_____

Thank You,
You are The Best Santa Ever!

Dear Santa:

My name is: ....

I am .... years old

I have been:
- ☐ Nice
- ☐ a lil bit naughty...but I can explain
- ☐ a bit of both

My christmas Wish List: ....

_____
_____
_____
_____

Thank you,
You are The Best Santa Ever!

Dear Santa:

My Name is: ....

I am .... Years old

I have been:
- ☐ Nice
- ☐ a lil bit naughty...but I can explain
- ☐ a bit of both

My Christmas Wish List: ....

_____

_____

_____

_____

Thank you,
You are The Best Santa Ever!

Dear Santa:

My Name is:......................................

I am............. years old

I have been:
- ☐ Nice
- ☐ a lil bit naughty...but I can explain
- ☐ a bit of both

My christmas Wish List:......................

_____

_____

_____

_____

Thank you,
You are The Best Santa Ever!

Dear Santa:

My Name is: ....

I am .... Years old

I have been:
- ☐ Nice
- ☐ a Lil bit naughty...but I can explain
- ☐ a bit of both

My Christmas Wish List: ....

_____

_____

_____

_____

Thank you,
You are The Best Santa Ever!

Dear Santa:

My name is: ★....................

I am............ years old

I have been:
- ☐ Nice
- ☐ a lil bit naughty...but I can explain
- ☐ a bit of both

My Christmas Wish List:....................

_____

_____

_____

Thank You,
You are The Best Santa Ever!

Dear Santa:

My Name is:........................

I am......... Years old

I have been: ☐ Nice

☐ a Lil bit naughty...but I can explain

☐ a bit of both

My christmas Wish List:................

Thank you,
You are The Best Santa Ever!

Dear Santa:

My Name is: ....

I am .... Years old

I have been:
- ☐ Nice
- ☐ a lil bit naughty...but I can explain
- ☐ a bit of both

My Christmas Wish List: ....

_____

_____

_____

_____

Thank You,
You are The Best Santa Ever!

Dear Santa:

My Name is:........................

I am............ years old

I have been:
- ☐ Nice
- ☐ a lil bit naughty...but I can explain
- ☐ a bit of both

My christmas Wish List:................

_____

_____

_____

_____

Thank you,
You are The Best Santa Ever!

Dear Santa:

My name is: ....

I am .... years old

I have been: ☐ Nice

☐ a lil bit naughty...but I can explain

☐ a bit of both

My Christmas Wish List: ....

_____

_____

_____

_____

Thank you,
You are the Best Santa Ever!

Dear Santa:

My Name is:.......................

I am.......... Years old

I have been: ☐ Nice

☐ a lil bit naughty...but I can explain

☐ a bit of both

My Christmas Wish List:..................

Thank You,
You are The Best Santa Ever!

Dear Santa:

My Name is: ....

I am .... years old

I have been:
- ☐ Nice
- ☐ a lil bit naughty...but I can explain
- ☐ a bit of both

My christmas Wish List: ....

_____

_____

_____

_____

Thank you,
You are The Best Santa Ever!

Dear Santa:

My Name is:........................

I am.........years old

I have been:
- ☐ Nice
- ☐ a lil bit naughty...but I can explain
- ☐ a bit of both

My Christmas Wish List:................

_____

_____

_____

_____

Thank you,
You are The Best Santa Ever!

Dear Santa:

My Name is: ....

I am .... Years Old

I have been:
- ☐ Nice
- ☐ a Lil bit naughty...but I can explain
- ☐ a bit of both

My Christmas Wish List: ....

_____

_____

_____

_____

Thank You,
You are The Best Santa Ever!

Dear Santa:

My Name is:..........................

I am.......... Years old

I have been:
- ☐ Nice
- ☐ a lil bit naughty...but I can explain
- ☐ a bit of both

My Christmas Wish List:..................

_____

_____

_____

_____

Thank You,
You are The Best Santa Ever!

Dear Santa:

My Name is: ....

I am .... Years old

I have been:
- ☐ Nice
- ☐ a lil bit naughty...but I can explain
- ☐ a bit of both

My Christmas Wish List: ....
_____
_____
_____
_____

Thank You,
You are The Best Santa Ever!

Dear Santa:

My Name is: ....

I am .... years old

I have been:
- ☐ Nice
- ☐ a lil bit naughty...but I can explain
- ☐ a bit of both

My Christmas Wish List: ....

_____

_____

_____

Thank You,
You are The Best Santa Ever!

Dear Santa:

My Name is:..........................

I am............Years old

I have been: ☐ Nice

☐ a Lil bit naughty...but I can explain

☐ a bit of both

My Christmas Wish List:..................

_____

_____

_____

_____

Thank You,
You are The Best Santa Ever!

Dear Santa:

My Name is:........................

I am.............. years old

I have been:
- ☐ Nice
- ☐ a lil bit naughty...but I can explain
- ☐ a bit of both

My Christmas Wish List:..................

_____

_____

_____

_____

Thank you,
You are The Best Santa Ever!

Dear Santa:

My Name is: ....

I am .... years old

I have been:
- ☐ Nice
- ☐ a lil bit naughty...but I can explain
- ☐ a bit of both

My Christmas Wish List: ....

_____

_____

_____

_____

Thank you,
You are The Best Santa Ever!

Dear Santa:

My Name is:........................

I am.......... Years old

I have been: ☐ Nice

☐ a Lil bit naughty...but I can explain

☐ a bit of both

My Christmas Wish List:................

Thank You,
You are The Best Santa Ever!

Dear Santa:

My Name is:..........................

I am............ years old

I have been:

☐ Nice

☐ a lil bit naughty...but I can explain

☐ a bit of both

My Christmas Wish List:..................

———————————————
———————————————
———————————————
———————————————

Thank you,
You are The Best Santa Ever!

Dear Santa:

My Name is:⋯⋯⋯⋯⋯⋯⋯⋯⋯⋯

I am⋯⋯⋯ Years old

I have been: ☐ Nice

☐ a Lil bit naughty...but I can explain

☐ a bit of both

My christmas Wish List:⋯⋯⋯⋯⋯

Thank You,
You are The Best Santa Ever!

Dear Santa:

My Name is:................................

I am............ years old

I have been:
- ☐ Nice
- ☐ a lil bit naughty...but I can explain
- ☐ a bit of both

My christmas Wish List:................

_____

_____

_____

_____

Thank you,
You are The Best Santa Ever!

Dear Santa:

My Name is: ....

I am .... Years Old

I have been:
- ☐ Nice
- ☐ a lil bit naughty...but I can explain
- ☐ a bit of both

My Christmas Wish List: ....

_____

_____

_____

_____

Thank You,
You are The Best Santa Ever!

Dear Santa:

My Name is:⋆........................

I am........ Years old

I have been: ☐ Nice

☐ a Lil bit naughty...but I can explain

☐ a bit of both

My christmas Wish List:..................

_____

_____

_____

Thank You,
You are The Best Santa Ever!

Dear Santa:

My Name is:..........................

I am............ years old

I have been:
- ☐ Nice
- ☐ a lil bit naughty...but I can explain
- ☐ a bit of both

My christmas Wish List:..................

_____

_____

_____

_____

Thank You,
You are The Best Santa Ever!

Dear Santa:

My Name is:..............................

I am............ Years old

I have been:
- ☐ Nice
- ☐ a lil bit naughty...but I can explain
- ☐ a bit of both

My christmas Wish List:..............

_____

_____

_____

_____

Thank You,
You are The Best Santa Ever!

Dear Santa:

My Name is:⋆........................

I am............ years old

I have been:
- ☐ Nice
- ☐ a lil bit naughty...but I can explain
- ☐ a bit of both

My Christmas Wish List:..................

_____

_____

_____

_____

Thank you,
You are The Best Santa Ever!

Dear Santa:

My Name is:...........................

I am........... Years old

I have been: ☐ Nice

☐ a Lil bit naughty...but I can explain

☐ a bit of both

My christmas Wish List:...................

_____

_____

_____

_____

Thank You,
You are The Best Santa Ever!

Dear Santa:

My Name is:........................

I am............ Years old

I have been: ☐ Nice

☐ a Lil bit naughty...but I can explain

☐ a bit of both

My Christmas Wish List:................

_____

_____

_____

Thank you,
You are The Best Santa Ever!

Dear Santa:

My Name is:..........................

I am............ Years old

I have been:
- ☐ Nice
- ☐ a Lil bit naughty...but I can explain
- ☐ a bit of both

My Christmas Wish List:..................

_____

_____

_____

_____

Thank You,
You are The Best Santa Ever!

Dear Santa:

My Name is: ....

I am .... Years old

I have been:
- ☐ Nice
- ☐ a Lil bit naughty...but I can explain
- ☐ a bit of both

My Christmas Wish List: ....

_____

_____

_____

_____

Thank You,
You are The Best Santa Ever!

Dear Santa:

My Name is:..............................

I am............ Years old

I have been:
- ☐ Nice
- ☐ a Lil bit naughty...but I can explain
- ☐ a bit of both

My Christmas Wish List:...................

_____

_____

_____

_____

Thank You,
You are The Best Santa Ever!

Dear Santa:

My Name is: ....

I am .... Years old

I have been:
- ☐ Nice
- ☐ a Lil bit naughty...but I can explain
- ☐ a bit of both

My Christmas Wish List: ....

_____

_____

_____

Thank You,
You are The Best Santa Ever!

Dear Santa:

My Name is:......................

I am............ Years old

I have been:

☐ Nice

☐ a Lil bit naughty...but I can explain

☐ a bit of both

My Christmas Wish List:..................

_____

_____

_____

_____

Thank You,
You are The Best Santa Ever!

Dear Santa:

My Name is:........................

I am............ Years old

I have been:
☐ Nice

☐ a Lil bit naughty...but I can explain

☐ a bit of both

My Christmas Wish List:................

_____

_____

_____

Thank You,
You are The Best Santa Ever!

Dear Santa:

My Name is:........................

I am............ Years old

I have been:
- ☐ Nice
- ☐ a lil bit naughty...but I can explain
- ☐ a bit of both

My Christmas Wish List:................

_____

_____

_____

_____

Thank You,
You are The Best Santa Ever!

Dear Santa:

My Name is:..............................

I am............ Years old

I have been: ☐ Nice

☐ a Lil bit naughty...but I can explain

☐ a bit of both

My Christmas Wish List:..................

_____

_____

_____

Thank You,
You are The Best Santa Ever!

Dear Santa:

My Name is:........................

I am............ Years old

I have been:
- ☐ Nice
- ☐ a Lil bit naughty...but I can explain
- ☐ a bit of both

My Christmas Wish List:................

_____
_____
_____
_____

Thank You,
You are The Best Santa Ever!

Dear Santa:

My Name is:............................

I am........... Years old

I have been:
☐ Nice
☐ a Lil bit naughty...but I can explain
☐ a bit of both

My Christmas Wish List:..................

_____

_____

_____

_____

Thank You,
You are The Best Santa Ever!

Dear Santa:

My Name is:........................

I am............ Years old

I have been: ☐ Nice

☐ a Lil bit naughty...but I can explain

☐ a bit of both

My Christmas Wish List:................

_____
_____
_____
_____

Thank You,
You are The Best Santa Ever!

Dear Santa:

My Name is:......................

I am............. Years old

I have been:
- ☐ Nice
- ☐ a Lil bit naughty...but I can explain
- ☐ a bit of both

My Christmas Wish List:...................

_____

_____

_____

_____

Thank You,
You are The Best Santa Ever!

Dear Santa:

My Name is:......................

I am........... Years old

I have been: ☐ Nice

☐ a Lil bit naughty...but I can explain

☐ a bit of both

My Christmas Wish List:................

Thank You,
You are The Best Santa Ever!

Dear Santa:

My Name is:....................

I am............ years old

I have been:
- ☐ Nice
- ☐ a lil bit naughty...but I can explain
- ☐ a bit of both

My Christmas Wish List:....................

_____

_____

_____

_____

Thank You,
You are The Best Santa Ever!

Dear Santa:

My Name is: ....

I am .... Years old

I have been:
- ☐ Nice
- ☐ a lil bit naughty...but I can explain
- ☐ a bit of both

My Christmas Wish List: ....

_____

_____

_____

_____

Thank You,
You are The Best Santa Ever!

Dear Santa:

My Name is:......................

I am........ Years old

I have been:
- ☐ Nice
- ☐ a Lil bit naughty...but I can explain
- ☐ a bit of both

My christmas Wish List:..................

_____

_____

_____

_____

Thank you,
You are The Best Santa Ever!

Dear Santa:

My Name is:.........................

I am............ Years old

I have been:
- ☐ Nice
- ☐ a lil bit naughty...but I can explain
- ☐ a bit of both

My Christmas Wish List:..................

_____
_____
_____
_____

Thank You,
You are The Best Santa Ever!

Dear Santa:

My Name is:....................

I am........ years old

I have been:
- ☐ Nice
- ☐ a lil bit naughty...but I can explain
- ☐ a bit of both

My Christmas Wish List:....................

_____

_____

_____

Thank you,
You are The Best Santa Ever!

Dear Santa:

My Name is:.........................

I am........ Years old

I have been:
- ☐ Nice
- ☐ a lil bit naughty...but I can explain
- ☐ a bit of both

My Christmas Wish List:..................

_____

_____

_____

_____

Thank You,
You are The Best Santa Ever!

Dear Santa:

My Name is:........................

I am......... Years old

I have been: ☐ Nice

☐ a lil bit naughty...but I can explain

☐ a bit of both

My Christmas Wish List:..................

_____

_____

_____

_____

Thank You,
You are The Best Santa Ever!

Dear Santa:

My Name is:......................

I am.......... Years old

I have been:
- ☐ Nice
- ☐ a Lil bit naughty...but I can explain
- ☐ a bit of both

My Christmas Wish List:..................

_____

_____

_____

_____

Thank You,
You are The Best Santa Ever!

Dear Santa:

My Name is:........................

I am............ Years Old

I have been: ☐ Nice

☐ a Lil bit Naughty...but I can explain

☐ a bit of both

My Christmas Wish List:................

_____

_____

_____

_____

Thank You,
You are The Best Santa Ever!

Dear Santa:

My Name is:..........................

I am.......... years old

I have been:
☐ Nice
☐ a Lil bit naughty...but I can explain
☐ a bit of both

My Christmas Wish List:..................

_____

_____

_____

_____

Thank You,
You are The Best Santa Ever!

Dear Santa:

My Name is: ....

I am .... years old

I have been: ☐ Nice

☐ a lil bit naughty...but I can explain

☐ a bit of both

My Christmas Wish List: ....

_____

_____

_____

_____

Thank you,
You are The Best Santa Ever!

Dear Santa:

My Name is: ....

I am .... years old

I have been:
- ☐ Nice
- ☐ a lil bit naughty...but I can explain
- ☐ a bit of both

My Christmas Wish List: ....

_____
_____
_____
_____

Thank You,
You are The Best Santa Ever!

Dear Santa:

My Name is: ....

I am .... years old

I have been:
- ☐ Nice
- ☐ a lil bit naughty...but I can explain
- ☐ a bit of both

My Christmas Wish List: ....

_____

_____

_____

Thank You,
You are The Best Santa Ever!

Dear Santa:

My Name is: ....

I am .... Years old

I have been:
- ☐ Nice
- ☐ a Lil bit naughty...but I can explain
- ☐ a bit of both

My Christmas Wish List: ....

_____

_____

_____

_____

Thank You,
You are The Best Santa Ever!

Dear Santa:

My Name is:..........................

I am........ years old

I have been:
- ☐ Nice
- ☐ a Lil bit naughty...but I can explain
- ☐ a bit of both

My Christmas Wish List:..................

_____

_____

_____

Thank You,
You are The Best Santa Ever!

Dear Santa:

My Name is:......................

I am............ years old

I have been:
- ☐ Nice
- ☐ a lil bit naughty...but I can explain
- ☐ a bit of both

My christmas Wish List:..................

_____

_____

_____

_____

Thank you,
You are The Best Santa Ever!

Dear Santa:

My Name is: ....

I am .... Years Old

I have been:
- ☐ Nice
- ☐ a Lil bit naughty...but I can explain
- ☐ a bit of both

My Christmas Wish List: ....

_____

_____

_____

Thank You,
You are The Best Santa Ever!

Dear Santa:

My Name is:..........................

I am............ years old

I have been: ☐ Nice

☐ a Lil bit naughty...but I can explain

☐ a bit of both

My Christmas Wish List:..................

_____

_____

_____

_____

Thank You,
You are The Best Santa Ever!

Dear Santa:

My Name is:..........................

I am.......... Years old

I have been:
- ☐ Nice
- ☐ a lil bit naughty...but I can explain
- ☐ a bit of both

My christmas Wish List:..................

_____

_____

_____

_____

Thank You,
You are The Best Santa Ever!

Dear Santa:

My Name is:........................

I am............ Years old

I have been:
☐ Nice

☐ a Lil bit naughty...but I can explain

☐ a bit of both

My christmas Wish List:................

_____

_____

_____

_____

Thank You,
You are The Best Santa Ever!

Dear Santa:

My Name is:........................

I am............ years old

I have been:
- ☐ Nice
- ☐ a lil bit naughty...but I can explain
- ☐ a bit of both

My Christmas Wish List:................

_____

_____

_____

_____

Thank you,
You are the Best Santa Ever!

Dear Santa:

My Name is:......................................

I am............ years old

I have been: ☐ Nice

☐ a lil bit naughty...but I can explain

☐ a bit of both

My christmas Wish List:....................

_____

_____

_____

_____

Thank You,
You are The Best Santa Ever!

Dear Santa:

My name is: ....

I am .... years old

I have been:
- ☐ Nice
- ☐ a lil bit naughty...but I can explain
- ☐ a bit of both

My Christmas Wish List: ....

_____

_____

_____

_____

Thank you,
You are the Best Santa Ever!

Dear Santa:

My Name is: ....

I am .... Years old

I have been: ☐ Nice

☐ a lil bit naughty...but I can explain

☐ a bit of both

My Christmas Wish List: ....

_____

_____

_____

_____

Thank You,
You are The Best Santa Ever!

Dear Santa:

My Name is:..........................

I am.......... Years old

I have been:
- ☐ Nice
- ☐ a Lil bit naughty...but I can explain
- ☐ a bit of both

My Christmas Wish List:..................

_____

_____

_____

Thank You,
You are The Best Santa Ever!

Dear Santa:

My Name is:⋆............................

I am............ years old

I have been:
- ☐ Nice
- ☐ a lil bit naughty...but I can explain
- ☐ a bit of both

My christmas Wish List:..................

_____

_____

_____

Thank you,
You are The Best Santa Ever!

Dear Santa:

My Name is:........................

I am............ Years old

I have been:
- ☐ Nice
- ☐ a lil bit naughty...but I can explain
- ☐ a bit of both

My Christmas Wish List:..................

_____

_____

_____

_____

Thank You,
You are The Best Santa Ever!

Dear Santa:

My Name is:⋆⋆⋆⋆⋆⋆⋆⋆⋆⋆⋆⋆⋆⋆⋆⋆⋆⋆⋆⋆

I am ⋆⋆⋆⋆⋆⋆⋆⋆ years old

I have been:

☐ Nice

☐ a lil bit naughty...but I can explain

☐ a bit of both

My Christmas Wish List:⋆⋆⋆⋆⋆⋆⋆⋆⋆⋆⋆⋆

_____

_____

_____

_____

Thank You,
You are The Best Santa Ever!

www.ingramcontent.com/pod-product-compliance
Lightning Source LLC
Chambersburg PA
CBHW081235080526
44587CB00022B/3945